CORNERSTONES OF FREEDOM™

The NUCLEAR AGE

BY PETER BENOIT

CHILDREN'S PRESS®

An Imprint of Scholastic Inc.

New York   Toronto   London   Auckland   Sydney
Mexico City   New Delhi   Hong Kong
Danbury, Connecticut

BRINGING HISTORY to LIFE

Content Consultant
James Marten, PhD
Professor and Chair, History Department
Marquette University
Milwaukee, Wisconsin

Library of Congress Cataloging-in-Publication Data
Benoit, Peter, 1955–
  The nuclear age/by Peter Benoit.
      p. cm.—(Cornerstones of freedom)
  Includes bibliographical references and index.
  Audience: Grades 4 to 6.
  ISBN-13: 978-0-531-23062-6 (lib. bdg.)   ISBN-10: 0-531-23062-7 (lib. bdg.)
  ISBN-13: 978-0-531-28162-8 (pbk.)   ISBN-10: 0-531-28162-0 (pbk.)
  1. Nuclear weapons—History—Juvenile literature. 2. Nuclear
energy—History—Juvenile literature. I. Title.
  U264.B452 2012
  355.02'17—dc23   2011031341

1 2 3 4 5 6 7 8 9 10 R 21 20 19 18 17 16 15 14 13 12

Photographs © 2012: AP Images: 23 (Clipper Today), 54 (Korean Central
News Agency via Korea News Service), 50 (Kyodo News), 46 (Lee Jin-
man), 44 (Mark Schiefelbein), 6 (North Wind Picture Archives), 5 bottom,
48 (PRNewsFoto/Westinghouse Electric Company), 4 bottom, 14, 57 top
(stf), 12 (William J. Smith), 5 top, 13, 25, 35, 39; Corbis Images: 37, 57 bottom,
59 (Hulton-Deutsch Collection), 2, 3, 34 (Roger Ressmeyer); Dreamstime:
cover (Kcphotos), back cover (Striver); Everett Collection: 40; Getty Images:
30 (Department Of Energy/Time & Life Pictures), 36 (Ed Clark/Time & Life
Pictures), 20 (Gamma-Keystone), 27 (Julius Buschel/Keystone), 55 (Junko
Kimura/Bloomberg), 15, 21 (Keystone/Stringer/Hulton Archive), 4 top, 10,
56 (March Of Time/Time & Life Pictures), 28 (Paul Schutzer/Time & Life
Pictures), 22 (PhotoQuest), 16 (Popperfoto), 47 (Sankei), 18 (US Army/Time
& Life Pictures); Granger Collection: 7, 29 (Rue des Archives), 8 (ullstein
bild); Shutterstock, Inc.: 41 (Nomad_Soul), 42 (Robert Fullerton); The Image
Works/RIA Novosti: 32, 49, 58;
U.S. Coast Guard: 33.

Maps by XNR Productions, Inc.

Did you know that studying history can be fun?

BRING HISTORY TO LIFE by becoming a history investigator. Examine the evidence (primary and secondary source materials); cross-examine the people and witnesses. Take a look at what was happening at the time—but be careful! What happened years ago might suddenly become incredibly interesting and change the way you think!

Contents

A Major Discovery

Henri Becquerel was one of the first scientists to discover radioactivity.

Several scientific discoveries in the late 1800s helped to create worldwide interest in nuclear power. The work of scientists such as Henri Becquerel and Marie Curie, who

HENRI BECQUEREL SHARED THE 1903 NOBEL PRIZE

discovered radioactivity in certain elements, caused other scientists to rethink what they knew about **atoms**. The work of Ernest Rutherford soon after gave scientists a deeper understanding of the atom. It suggested that the atomic **nucleus** possessed its own powerful energy.

The question of how best to use that energy has occupied scientists and world leaders ever since. Starting in the 1950s, nuclear energy

Ernest Rutherford's work on radioactivity won him the 1908 Nobel Prize in Chemistry.

has traveled two paths. It can be used as an inexpensive source of electricity. But it can also be used as an incredibly destructive weapon. Nuclear energy has both benefits and risks. Debates about nuclear energy have shaped politics and changed the way we think about the world. But at the beginning of the 20th century, nuclear energy was still a new discovery with a great deal of potential. Scientists around the world worked tirelessly to find out more about the new energy source.

THE BIRTH OF A NEW AGE

German scientists Otto Hahn (right) and Lise Meitner (left) were among the first to experiment with nuclear fission.

A NEW UNDERSTANDING OF the atomic nucleus began to take shape in the 1930s. Scientists discovered that it was made up of tiny pieces called protons and neutrons. An attractive force held the protons and neutrons together tightly. Scientists began trying to split a uranium nucleus by launching neutrons into it. They believed that the nucleus would break into smaller nuclei. This process of a nucleus breaking apart would later be called **nuclear fission**. In 1939, chemists in Germany succeeded in breaking a nucleus apart. They learned that successful fission released a great deal of energy. Some saw this energy's potential as a weapon. Among them were Nazi German scientists.

Albert Einstein (left) and Leo Szilard (right) used their influence to convince President Roosevelt of the importance of nuclear weapons research.

The Beginning of the Bomb

International conflict broke out in Europe in 1939. Nazi leader and German führer Adolf Hitler began an assault on Czechoslovakia on March 15.

Many scientists had fled Germany several years earlier so that they would not be forced to help the Nazis. Among them was physicist Leo Szilard. Szilard knew that Nazi Germany had begun a nuclear weapons research project. He and two fellow scientists carefully drafted a letter to the president of the United States on August 2. It warned of the Nazis' plans and urged U.S.

president Franklin Delano Roosevelt to develop nuclear weapons. Szilard approached his friend and fellow physicist Albert Einstein to ask for his support. Einstein agreed. A handful of scientists worked together on the letter, but in the end only Einstein signed it.

The Einstein-Szilard letter led to the beginning of fission research in the United States. Roosevelt did not see the letter until October 11. He responded on October 19. Hitler invaded Poland a little more than a week later. World War II had officially begun. Japan would eventually join with Germany, Italy, and other countries to form the Axis powers. Russia, Great Britain, the United States, and many others would form the Allied forces.

Roosevelt called for the formation of an Advisory Committee on Uranium. The committee set aside $6,000 for basic research. Researchers at first believed that tons of uranium might be necessary to make an atomic bomb. Great Britain's bomb committee estimated instead that very small amounts would be enough. They pointed to the practical aspects of using the bomb in battle. They detailed the amount of radiation that would be released

A FIRSTHAND LOOK AT
THE EINSTEIN-SZILARD LETTER

The Einstein-Szilard letter informed President Franklin Roosevelt of Nazi nuclear weapons research. It also led to fission research in the United States and spawned the Manhattan Project. See page 60 for a link to read the letter online.

Dr. Vannevar Bush served as director of the Office of Scientific Research and Development.

and argued for the need to develop an atomic bomb before the Axis powers did. The smaller uranium estimate proposed by the British raised the possibility of building a bomb small enough to be dropped from an airplane.

Roosevelt created the Office of Scientific Research and Development (OSRD) in June 1941 to support scientific research for national defense. The OSRD researched radar and warning systems. It also researched regular weapons and wartime medical treatment. One highly secretive division was entrusted with the development of a uranium bomb.

As research began, Great Britain complained frequently that U.S. researchers were not making enough progress. But the United States was soon given good reason to speed up the development of a nuclear bomb. In late 1941, the United States was pulled into World War II. Japan attacked the U.S. military base at Pearl Harbor, Hawaii, on December 7. Germany declared war on the United States a few days later.

Around 2,300 Americans were killed in the attack on Pearl Harbor.

Brigadier General Leslie Groves (right) served as the Manhattan Project's military director. Physicist J. Robert Oppenheimer (left) served as the project's scientific director.

The Manhattan Project

The OSRD began to work closely with the U.S. Army in 1942. The Manhattan Project was established in June and headed by Brigadier General Leslie Groves. The Manhattan Project worked to develop the uranium bomb and monitor the German nuclear program. U.S. scientists worked closely with Great Britain and Canada at dozens of sites spread across the three nations. The United States assumed a leadership role in the project, and the U.S. Army assumed full control by 1943.

Scientists soon decided that it would be too expensive to build a uranium bomb. They began working with plutonium instead. The Army Corps of Engineers began building **nuclear reactors** to make plutonium. Construction was soon completed and plutonium production began. The first plutonium was delivered to Los Alamos National Laboratory in New Mexico in early 1945. On July 16, Manhattan Project engineers detonated a test bomb called Trinity near Alamogordo, New Mexico. The explosion was heard more than 200 miles (322 kilometers) away. Desert sands melted and turned to radioactive green glass as a mushroom cloud rose more than 3 miles (4.8 km) into the air. It was the beginning of the nuclear age.

YESTERDAY'S HEADLINES

Kamikaze attacks caused a great deal of damage to the Allied military forces during World War II. In these attacks, Japanese planes were loaded with explosives and the pilots crashed them into targets. Attacks by Japan's suicide pilots peaked in the Battle of Okinawa in June 1945. More than 50,000 Allied troops were killed or wounded in the battle. But Japanese losses were even greater. Almost 200,000 Japanese troops were killed or wounded. The Allies' victory was costly. But it preserved the option of a massive invasion of Japan as an alternative to using the bomb.

Szilard and 69 cosigners submitted a petition to President Harry S. Truman the next morning. They urged him to think carefully before using the atomic bomb to end the war in Japan. Truman discussed using the bomb with Generals Omar Bradley and Dwight Eisenhower on July 20. Eisenhower spoke against such a plan. He believed that the war could be won without resorting to the bomb. He suggested that the Japanese were already almost defeated. They would likely surrender soon. But Truman saw the matter differently.

B-29 bombers had destroyed more than half of Tokyo. The remains of the Imperial Japanese Navy lay on the floor of the Pacific Ocean. But Japan continued the fight against all odds. It launched kamikaze attacks and sank

A single atomic bomb completely destroyed the city of Hiroshima.

34 American aircraft carriers in the months following Pearl Harbor. Thousands of lives were lost. Truman believed that Japan might continue fighting for a year or more. A full-scale invasion of Japan to convince them to surrender would be paid for in American lives. It was predicted that more than 250,000 troops could be lost in such an attack. Truman was faced with a crucial decision.

The United States dropped an atomic bomb on Hiroshima, Japan, on August 6, 1945. A second atomic bomb was dropped on the city of Nagasaki three days later. More than 200,000 Japanese citizens died in the two bombings. Some were killed directly by the blast. Others died as a result of injuries or radiation poisoning. The Japanese assumed that a third atomic bomb was coming when regular air attacks began again. There was none. Japanese emperor Hirohito chose to surrender on August 15. One war was coming to an end. But a very different one was about to begin.

A FIRSTHAND LOOK AT
HIROSHIMA PHOTOGRAPHS

President Truman's decision to unleash nuclear attacks on Hiroshima and Nagasaki may have spared hundreds of thousands of American lives. But it caused incredible devastation to Japan. Photographs of the aftermath in Hiroshima show just how much damage the bombs did. See page 60 for a link to view photos of Hiroshima online.

COLD WAR

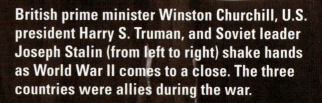

British prime minister Winston Churchill, U.S. president Harry S. Truman, and Soviet leader Joseph Stalin (from left to right) shake hands as World War II comes to a close. The three countries were allies during the war.

THE MANHATTAN PROJECT AND

the rise of nuclear weapons influenced international politics for many years after the first bomb was dropped. The period from the end of World War II to the collapse of the Soviet Union in 1991 was marked by political conflict and competition between the Soviet Union and the United States. But military tension never grew into open combat between the two nations. The battles of this Cold War were fought in more subtle ways. One of the biggest struggles of the period was over nuclear **proliferation**. Nuclear war appeared likely many times throughout the Cold War. But both countries knew that a nuclear attack would result in destruction for both of them.

Physicist and spy Klaus Fuchs passed information about the Manhattan Project to Soviet scientists.

The Soviet Threat

At the end of World War II, many people believed that the Soviet Union was close to creating its own nuclear weapons. U.S. scientists pushed for diplomacy, or peaceful cooperation, with the Soviets to prevent a nuclear showdown. But Truman's cabinet of advisers voted for research to proceed on an even more powerful bomb. The device would be able to release far more energy than the fission bombs used in Japan.

U.S. agents arrested a man named Klaus Fuchs in early 1950. Fuchs had worked on the Manhattan Project. But he was now revealed to be a Soviet spy. Truman pushed to continue research on the new bomb. In

November 1952, the United States detonated the first thermonuclear bomb, also called the hydrogen bomb, in a remote part of the Pacific Ocean. The bomb used extremely high temperatures to set off a chain reaction in the bomb's hydrogen, causing the atoms to combine to create helium. The result was a highly explosive force that could be 1,000 times more destructive than a fission bomb. Now the United States was ahead of the Soviets in nuclear weapons. This encouraged the Soviets to work even harder to win the nuclear arms race, and they detonated their first hydrogen bomb less than 10 months later.

Nuclear weapons were being produced at an amazing pace in both countries. The public was alarmed by the

The first hydrogen bomb test explosion created a cloud of smoke and radioactivity that covered thousands of square miles.

Fallout shelters were stocked with canned and boxed foods that would not spoil.

risks that the new military technology created. Both the Soviet and American governments worked to improve civil defense programs. Each country's program was designed to protect the country in case of attack. The basements of thousands of buildings across the United States were converted into **fallout** shelters. They were stocked with food and drinking water. City authorities developed evacuation plans in the event of a nuclear attack.

On December 12, 1958, the federal government began building a huge underground complex at the suggestion of President Eisenhower. This very expensive complex was located deep beneath the Greenbrier resort in White Sulphur Springs, West Virginia. The secret bunker was large enough to house all three branches of the federal government. That way, the country's government could remain safe during a nuclear attack.

Private citizens also built their own shelters. Schools across America conducted air-raid drills. Students practiced what to do to survive an attack. These efforts did very little to ease the minds of the public. Many Americans were also frustrated by the expense of the nuclear weapons program. The United States and Soviet Union continued to build more nuclear weapons. This eventually became a drain on their national economies. It contributed to the collapse of the Soviet Union in 1991. In the United States, nuclear defense spending took hundreds of billions of dollars from education and programs for the poor.

Students were taught to "duck and cover" during air-raid drills.

"Atoms for Peace"

President Eisenhower knew he needed to address the concerns of the American people. He delivered a speech before the United Nations on December 8, 1953. It came to be known as "Atoms for Peace." The Soviet detonation of a thermonuclear bomb a few months before had highlighted the importance of avoiding a nuclear war. Eisenhower proposed the creation of a United Nations nuclear bank. The United States and the Soviet Union would each set aside some nuclear material for peaceful purposes. The Soviets were not interested in this plan.

Eisenhower also realized that introducing nuclear energy into Western Europe would strengthen bonds between the United States and its allies. In a classified National Security Council Report from April 14, 1950, the United States had established a Cold War strategy of "containment." But nuclear reactors that used uranium to produce nuclear energy could also be used to prepare it for nuclear weapons. This meant that the export of peaceful nuclear technology could be a way of

A FIRSTHAND LOOK AT
EISENHOWER'S "ATOMS FOR PEACE" SPEECH

President Eisenhower outlined a plan to promote the peaceful use of nuclear power in a 1953 address before the United Nations. Eisenhower's speech also lent support to nuclear reactor technology as a source of energy. See page 60 for a link to read the speech online.

President Eisenhower (second from left) worked closely with other government officials to come up with a new plan for using nuclear power.

establishing anti-Soviet influence in the Soviet Union's neighboring countries. More countries would have access to nuclear weapons technology and tensions would continue to grow between the Soviet Union and the United States and its allies. The speech added to the worsening problem of nuclear proliferation.

Eisenhower's speech began a new way of thinking about nuclear technology. Supporters of nuclear power saw its potential to produce inexpensive electricity. They also saw that nuclear power could reduce the pollution

caused by burning fossil fuels such as coal and oil. Nuclear chemistry had potential for medical uses. Irradiation of food could extend its shelf life.

The Soviets had begun using nuclear power for electricity in 1954. Surpassing the Soviets in the new technology fit in well with the competitive nature of the Cold War. The first American nuclear-powered submarine was built in September 1954. It was named USS *Nautilus*. The Shippingport Atomic Power Station was producing electricity commercially by December 1957. The International Atomic Energy Agency (IAEA) was established in July 1957 to promote nuclear science and technology and its safe use. More and more nuclear reactors were built throughout the 1960s.

Nuclear power soon came to be viewed as a benefit to countries wishing to produce inexpensive energy. It was also seen as a growing danger because of the proliferation of nuclear weapons. The threat of nuclear destruction was never far from the public consciousness, even in peacetime. It sometimes took center stage in tense confrontations between the Soviet Union and the United States and its allies.

The two superpowers often supported smaller nations to gain strategic advantages over each other. They offered supplies and economic aid to these nations.

Representatives from more than 80 countries participated in the IAEA when it was first established. There are more than 135 member countries today.

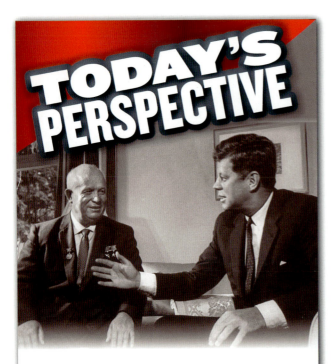

TODAY'S PERSPECTIVE

Cuban leader Fidel Castro was furious with Soviet leader Nikita Khrushchev (left) for backing down during the Cuban missile crisis. But Castro remained a Soviet ally. The Soviet people saw Khrushchev's actions as an act of weakness. He was forced out of office two years later. They did not know that Khrushchev had won an important victory by convincing President Kennedy (right) to remove U.S. missiles from Turkey.

Many people viewed the resolution to the crisis as Kennedy's finest hour. But Dean Acheson, who was a member of Kennedy's executive advisory committee during the crisis, called it "plain dumb luck."

Hostilities between the United States and Soviet Union reached the boiling point dangerously close to American shores in October 1962. President John F. Kennedy was alerted that a U.S. spy plane had taken photographs of a missile launch site in Cuba. The Soviets were preparing to attack American cities. Kennedy was in a difficult bind. He would lose the respect of European allies if he ordered a military strike against Cuba. He instead ordered a naval **blockade** of Cuban ports. Kennedy readied American military forces for invasion in case the blockade erupted in violence.

In the meantime, Kennedy engaged

President Kennedy's announcement of the naval blockade against Cuba was a major news event in 1962.

Soviet leader Nikita Khrushchev in negotiations for the removal of the Cuban missiles. He offered to remove U.S. missiles from Turkey. Khrushchev agreed to Kennedy's terms, and the crisis was averted. Kennedy agreed in return to recognize Cuba as an independent nation.

Nuclear weapons were never used during the 45 years of the Cold War. But their threatening presence shaped political alliances and the course of history in lasting ways.

CHAPTER 3

THE ATOM'S LEGACY

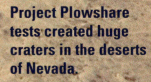

Project Plowshare tests created huge craters in the deserts of Nevada.

EISENHOWER'S UNITED

Nations address in 1953 had reminded the world that the greatness of nuclear power lay in its ability to "serve the peaceful pursuits of mankind." But building nuclear reactors is expensive and takes time. Edward Teller was a Hungarian physicist who had worked on the Manhattan Project. He suggested using peaceful explosions for large construction projects. He suggested that **excavations** and building canals, which both required moving large amounts of earth, would be made easier with underground nuclear blasts.

Project Plowshare was created in 1958 to research this idea. Scientists hoped to use nuclear blasts for dozens of large civil engineering projects. But test blasts always left lethal levels of radiation. Project Plowshare was eventually ended in 1975.

The world's first nuclear power plant was built in the Soviet city of Obninsk.

New Uses for Nuclear Technology

The Soviets began two similar programs under the title Nuclear Explosions for the National Economy in 1965. Controlled nuclear blasts were used for canal construction. They were also used for building toxic waste storage sites and successfully closing gas wells. But the Soviet program ended up creating too much radiation to be practical. The Soviets abandoned these programs by 1989.

In 2010, the BP oil company officials failed repeatedly to cap the Deepwater Horizon oil spill in the Gulf of Mexico. Some remembered the successes the Soviets had in closing gas wells with nuclear explosions years before, and considered it for this disaster. But this plan would have violated arms treaties. The idea was quickly set aside.

Many new reactors were built in the second half of the twentieth century. Nuclear power gradually became the main source of electricity worldwide. Some people began local antinuclear movements. The first one began in 1958 when Pacific Gas & Electric proposed building a nuclear power plant in Bodega Bay, California. The

Some people hoped that small nuclear explosions could help close gas wells during the 2010 Deepwater Horizon oil spill.

plant would have been built on the San Andreas Fault, putting it in danger of damage from earthquakes. Its construction also risked harming the local fishing and dairy farming industries. The battle raged on for six years until the project was finally abandoned in 1964.

Attempts to build a reactor in Malibu, California, were also met with vocal opposition. The nuclear industry was defeated once again. Pacific Gas & Electric finally won the battle to build a reactor in Avila Beach, California. The Diablo Canyon Power Plant began operating in May 1985 after years of legal challenges and antinuclear protests.

The Diablo Canyon Power Plant is located on the coast of the Pacific Ocean.

Thousands of activists worked to prevent the construction of the Seabrook Station Nuclear Power Plant in New Hampshire.

Protests

Media coverage of the protests served to focus attention on the nuclear debate. It became common for protesters to camp out illegally at reactor construction sites. Demonstrators and activists at the Seabrook Station Nuclear Power Plant on the New Hampshire coast managed to delay the completion of the plant for nearly two decades. In other cases, protesters caused power companies to completely scrap their plans for reactors.

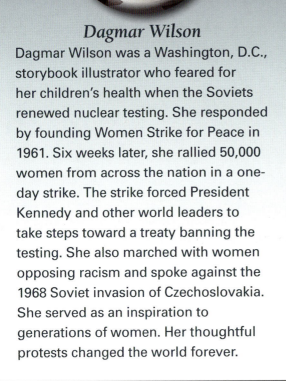

Dagmar Wilson

Dagmar Wilson was a Washington, D.C., storybook illustrator who feared for her children's health when the Soviets renewed nuclear testing. She responded by founding Women Strike for Peace in 1961. Six weeks later, she rallied 50,000 women from across the nation in a one-day strike. The strike forced President Kennedy and other world leaders to take steps toward a treaty banning the testing. She also marched with women opposing racism and spoke against the 1968 Soviet invasion of Czechoslovakia. She served as an inspiration to generations of women. Her thoughtful protests changed the world forever.

Protesters were especially opposed to nuclear weapons. Women Strike for Peace formed under the leadership of Congresswoman Bella Abzug and Dagmar Wilson in opposition to Soviet nuclear tests. Support for the movement grew nationwide when the U.S. military pledged to restart its own nuclear tests. The organization pointed out that radioactive material had begun to appear in milk. The women insisted that nuclear testing was an issue affecting family life in the United States. The group gained credibility with petitions, Congressional **lobbies**, and lawsuits. On November 1, 1961, some 50,000 members of the group marched in peaceful protest in dozens of cities across the nation. Their voices were heard. The Soviet Union, the

United States, and the United Kingdom signed a treaty outlawing certain kinds of nuclear testing less than two years later.

Citizens and political leaders were concerned about the dangers of nuclear testing. But they were far more worried about the spread of nuclear technology. The advance of the arms race between the United States and Soviet Union raised new threats during the 1960s. Nations wishing to build nuclear reactors for peaceful ends were looked upon with suspicion. Those reactors could also be used to produce material for bombs. But blocking access to nuclear technology completely could

The United States, United Kingdom, and Soviet Union signed the Nuclear Test Ban Treaty in 1963.

hurt developing economies abroad. The Treaty on the Non-Proliferation of Nuclear Weapons was put in place in March 1970. It was an important step toward nuclear regulation.

The first nations to support the treaty were the United States, the Soviet Union, the United Kingdom, France, and China. Countries that already have nuclear weapons when they sign the treaty are forbidden to transfer the weapons to other nations. Countries that do not have nuclear weapons when they sign the treaty are not allowed to acquire or develop them. The treaty does not bar access to nuclear energy for peaceful purposes. It instead provides regulation of reactor technology to ensure that treaty nations do not use reactors to make uranium for weapons.

Nuclear activities are monitored to keep countries from violating the treaty. The United States Nuclear Regulatory Commission was formed on January 19, 1975. It oversees the treaty, and it licenses, inspects, and enforces its requirements at nuclear power plants. Critics of the commission claim that it has repeatedly failed to supervise the nuclear industry and has exposed citizens to unnecessary risks. They believe the commission should be reformed.

Meltdowns

The commission's failures have occasionally had dramatic and far-reaching consequences. On March 28, 1979, failure of pumps at the Three Mile Island (TMI) Nuclear Generating Station near Harrisburg,

The meltdown at Three Mile Island, in Pennsylvania, set off a new round of public concern over the safety of nuclear power.

YESTERDAY'S HEADLINES

A movie titled *The China Syndrome* opened in theaters just 12 days before the Three Mile Island (TMI) disaster occurred. The timing of the movie's release caused it to have a major effect on public opinion of nuclear power. The movie detailed the events of a nuclear meltdown. It showed how radiation could cause severe damage to the area around a power plant after a meltdown. The TMI meltdown was contained with minimal radiation leakage. But the public had been frightened by what they saw in the movie. They believed the accident at TMI had been far worse than it actually was.

Pennsylvania caused pressure and temperatures in the generator to rise to dangerous levels. The failure of a relief valve to open and close properly contributed to a partial **meltdown** of the reactor core. The reactor vessel itself did not fail, and radiation was well contained. But the tense days after the accident increased fears that nuclear technology could never be perfectly safe.

TMI stopped the nuclear industry in its tracks. Antinuclear feelings spread across the country. In 1986, explosions at the Soviets' Chernobyl nuclear power plant sent waves of fear around the globe. The Chernobyl explosions and widespread contamination raised old concerns about

Radiation from the Chernobyl meltdown severely damaged the land surrounding the power plant.

public health. The effect on the nuclear power industry was devastating. Chernobyl has also had a negative economic impact on the present-day countries of Ukraine and nearby Belarus. Prime agricultural land can no longer be used to grow crops.

Even with such concerns, about 20 percent of the electricity in the United States is generated by nuclear power. There are currently 104 reactors in use. The debate over whether more should be built rages on today. Both sides raise important arguments. There will be no easy answers.

CHAPTER 4

A HUMAN DILEMMA

Coal-burning power plants release large amounts of harmful gas into the atmosphere.

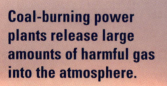

NUCLEAR ENERGY IS OFTEN THE focus of controversy. But many consider it our best solution to the problem of rising energy demand. Between 1970 and 2005, the demand for oil, gas, coal, and electricity increased significantly. This increase is expected to continue in the future. Growing demand for electricity is a major part of that growth. This is cause for alarm. Burning coal generates half the United States' electrical supply. But it also accounts for much of the **greenhouse gases** that are released into the air. These gases can cause damage to the environment.

Powerful storms such as the tornado that devastated Joplin, Missouri, in May 2011 could become more common as a result of climate change.

A Cleaner Source of Energy

Carbon dioxide is a greenhouse gas. Greenhouse gases collect in the atmosphere above Earth. They capture solar energy near Earth's surface, keeping Earth warm and allowing living things to exist. But too much of this can result in global **climate change**. Rising temperatures can cause deserts to increase in size. These deserts can overtake useful farmland. Climate change can also cause ice in colder areas to melt. The melted ice can cause sea levels to rise. Powerful ocean currents that distribute heat and affect the weather are altered. Destructive storms may become more common.

Some researchers have suggested using available technologies to capture some of the carbon dioxide produced by power plants before it enters the atmosphere. The gas would then be stored deep beneath Earth's surface or in ocean depths. But carbon capture at power plants could double the cost of producing electricity. It would also increase the amount of fuel the plant requires by as much as 40 percent. The plant would produce more carbon dioxide than it was removing. Nuclear plants might be a better option. They produce no greenhouse gases.

Decision makers must consider both the economy and the environment. A power plant generally lasts about 40 years, whether it uses coal, natural gas, or nuclear energy. The Nuclear Regulatory Commission licenses most power plants' reactors for exactly 40 years. Sixty-six of the nuclear reactors in the United States have had licenses extended another 20 years. Sixteen more are being considered for renewal. Twenty new plants are set to open over the next several years.

A FIRSTHAND LOOK AT
THE NUCLEAR REGULATORY COMMISSION

The Nuclear Regulatory Commission (NRC) is responsible for evaluating reactors for renewal. They also license new reactors. The NRC has specific guidelines for making their decisions. See page 60 for a link to view the guidelines online.

Building a power plant is very expensive. The average cost of building one new reactor for a new plant in the United States is between $6 billion and $8 billion. Investing in energy production assumes that the plant will produce high levels of electricity throughout its lifetime. The plant is only a good investment if it remains free of problems.

Deaths resulting directly from accidents are very uncommon at nuclear plants. Safety records show that deaths from accidents are actually more common at power plants that use fossil fuels such as coal or oil. But nuclear accidents attract a much larger amount of media attention than accidents at other power plants. This is in part because a nuclear meltdown can have far-reaching effects on the environment. Nuclear accidents and radiation leaks

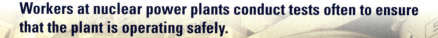

Workers at nuclear power plants conduct tests often to ensure that the plant is operating safely.

Cleanup workers wear special protective gear and use equipment to measure radiation at nuclear accident sites.

also can increase the risk of cancer in nearby populations. Another problem is that the Cold War caused many people to closely associate nuclear energy with nuclear weapons.

Nuclear power and nuclear weapons are very closely related in how they are made. The first step to making a nuclear bomb requires uranium. This uranium is used to make the plutonium that powers the bomb. Certain kinds of nuclear reactors used to create energy are able to make more plutonium than they use. This means they can produce energy even as they create the materials

New Reactor Designs

New reactor designs include safety features to protect the reactor core against meltdown. They are meant to avoid meltdowns even in the event of a total loss of electricity. They do not require humans to operate them. The Westinghouse AP1000 is one such reactor. It has received approval from the Nuclear Regulatory Commission. The AP1000 has systems that automatically respond to pressure changes, airflow, and gravity. This design is safer than previous models. But the superheated water it uses ruins pipes and joints rapidly. This means the pipes and joints will have to be inspected and replaced regularly.

needed to build nuclear weapons. The United States does not use any of these reactors. But they are currently used in Russia, China, India, and Japan.

The United States also bans the use of **spent uranium** to create materials for nuclear weapons. This is done in agreement with the country's position on nonproliferation. Using spent uranium allows more energy to be taken from uranium. It also reduces the amount of nuclear waste that is produced. But it moves away from nonproliferation and makes nuclear arms treaties more difficult to enforce. Any nuclear waste produced by the power plant must be stored safely to prevent radiation leaks. This adds to the risk and expense of producing nuclear energy and takes away some of the benefits of nuclear power.

New technology helps nuclear workers keep a close eye on everything that happens at power plants so they can prevent any potential accidents.

Meltdowns at nuclear power plants are rare. But they add to public mistrust of reactor technology. New reactor designs have better safety features and simpler designs. These new features are meant to prevent situations like those that occurred at TMI and Chernobyl. But some people point out that a simple malfunction is not the only risk to reactors.

Japan's Fukushima Nuclear Power Plant was hit by a magnitude 9.0 earthquake and a tsunami on March 11,

The earthquake and tsunami of March 2011 caused massive damage throughout Japan, including at more than one nuclear plant.

2011. Waves up to 46 feet (14 meters) high crashed onto Japan's coast. They flooded the reactor complex and cut off the electrical power necessary to operate the pumps. The reactor core began to overheat because it wasn't getting coolant from the pipes. The resulting meltdown could not be controlled. The surrounding area had to be evacuated. The accident caused widespread environmental damage. Other reactors around the world have also been built in areas where earthquakes are likely.

The Fukushima nuclear disaster points out the critical importance of choosing reactor sites with care. It also shows the importance of designing reactors to withstand any events they are likely to encounter. But it is impossible to imagine all of the risks.

Nuclear power filled a generation with high hopes for inexpensive energy. Now that dream has been tarnished. Only now do we understand its true costs and unique benefits. The choice of how to best use nuclear power is certain to be enormously difficult.

A VIEW FROM ABROAD

The Fukushima nuclear disaster has had a chilling effect on the nuclear industry worldwide. The biggest effect of all may have been in Germany. On May 30, 2011, Germany announced plans to close eight nuclear plants immediately. It also planned to close its nine remaining plants by 2022. This was a startling and bold declaration for a country that gets about 23 percent of its electricity from nuclear power. Germany plans to pioneer large-scale operations using solar and wind energy instead. Many Germans hope that this will lead to a technological revolution abroad. Others argue that the end of the nuclear power industry will harm Germany's industrial economy.

What Happened Where?

UNITED STATES

■ Three Mile Island

● Alamogordo

ATLANTIC OCEAN

Alamogordo, New Mexico The first nuclear bomb, called Trinity, was detonated in the desert outside this New Mexico town. This bomb proved to the scientists of the Manhattan Project that they had discovered how to build an atomic weapon capable of ending the war.

Three Mile Island The partial meltdown of Pennsylvania's Three Mile Island nuclear power plant in 1979 added to the public's fear of nuclear power. Even though the accident was largely contained, many people began to distrust the safety of nuclear plants.

ARCTIC OCEAN

Chernobyl The 1986 meltdown at the Chernobyl nuclear power plant in the Soviet Union was the worst nuclear accident in history. Radiation spread into the surrounding area and caused massive environmental damage.

Fukushima In 2011, a magnitude 9.0 earthquake and a tsunami hit Japan. The damage caused a meltdown at Fukushima power plant, and the surrounding area had to be evacuated.

Chernobyl
UKRAINE

JAPAN
Fukushima
Hiroshima
Nagasaki

PACIFIC OCEAN

Hiroshima and Nagasaki The United States dropped nuclear bombs on these two Japanese cities in 1945 in order to help end World War II. Hundreds of thousands of Japanese civilians were killed in the attacks. No nuclear bombs have been used in combat since.

INDIAN OCEAN

N
W   E
S

0   1,500   3,000 mi

0   1,500   3,000 km

An Uncertain Future

Nuclear powers such as North Korea, led by Kim Jong-il (center), are seen as a potential danger because of their refusal to sign the Nuclear Non-Proliferation Treaty.

Nuclear energy is only as safe as the countries are that take great care to use it responsibly. Its power cannot be taken lightly. North Korea has promised to expand its nuclear weapons arsenal. It has not signed the Nuclear

NORTH KOREA TESTED ITS FIRST

Non-Proliferation Treaty. India and Pakistan possess nuclear weapons but also have not signed the treaty. Israel has not signed the treaty either, and is widely believed to have nuclear weapons.

Iran's leaders deny that their reactors are being used to make materials for nuclear arms. They point to the importance of nuclear energy to meet the nation's growing needs. Many nations are thought to possess the knowledge needed to manufacture nuclear weapons. This makes regulation of nuclear material more important than ever before.

Nuclear power's unique benefits of creating inexpensive energy without producing greenhouse gases must be acknowledged. Regular energy technologies carry risks such as climate change and environmental pollution. While nuclear energy might be the best choice for the future, it carries with it fear and uncertainty.

Many people continue to protest against the use of nuclear power today.

INFLUENTIAL INDIVIDUALS

Albert Einstein

Albert Einstein (1879–1955) was the most famous physicist of the 20th century. The 1939 letter he wrote with Leo Szilard set in motion the fission research that made the creation of the atomic bomb possible.

Franklin Delano Roosevelt (1882–1945) was the 32nd president of the United States. He steered the nation through the Great Depression and World War II.

Harry S. Truman (1884–1972) was the 33rd president of the United States. He made the decision to use nuclear bombs in Japan to quickly end World War II in the Pacific.

Adolf Hitler (1889–1945) was the German chancellor from 1933 to 1945 and leader of the Nazi Party.

Dwight D. Eisenhower (1890–1969) was a World War II general and the 34th president of the United States. He delivered the "Atoms for Peace" speech to the United Nations.

Nikita Khrushchev (1894–1971) was first secretary of the Soviet Communist Party. He tested President Kennedy in October 1962 during the Cuban missile crisis.

Leslie Groves (1896–1970) was the U.S. lieutenant general who led the Manhattan Project.

Dagmar Wilson (1916–2011) was a peace activist and a protester against nuclear testing who founded Women Strike for Peace in 1961.

John F. Kennedy (1917–1963) was the 35th president of the United States. His diplomacy helped peacefully resolve the Cuban missile crisis.

Fidel Castro (1926–) was secretary-general of the Communist Party of Cuba. He opposed Khrushchev's negotiations with Kennedy during the Cuban missile crisis.

Leslie Groves

John F. Kennedy

TIMELINE

1939

March
Hitler invades Czechoslovakia.

August
Einstein, Szilard, and other scientists draft a letter to the president.

1941

June
Roosevelt creates the Office of Scientific Research and Development.

December
Japan attacks Pearl Harbor, and Germany declares war on the United States.

1942

June
The Manhattan Project begins.

1945

June
More than 50,000 Allied troops are killed or wounded in the Battle of Okinawa.

July 16
The test bomb, Trinity, is detonated.

1954

March
The Soviet Union opens its first plant to generate electricity from nuclear power.

1957

July
The International Atomic Energy Agency is established.

1962

October
The Cuban missile crisis brings the Cold War close to the American shore.

1970

March
The Nuclear Non-Proliferation Treaty goes into effect.

1945

August 6 and 9
The United States bombs Hiroshima and Nagasaki.

August 15
Japan surrenders in World War II.

1946–1991

The Soviet Union and the United States engage in the Cold War.

1952

November
The United States tests the first thermonuclear bomb.

1953

August
The Soviet Union detonates its first hydrogen bomb.

December 8
Eisenhower delivers his "Atoms for Peace" speech before the United Nations.

1975

January
The Nuclear Regulatory Commission is formed.

1979

March 28
A reactor core at the Three Mile Island nuclear plant partially melts down.

1986

April 25
Chernobyl melts down.

2011

March
Fukushima melts down.

LIVING HISTORY

Primary sources provide firsthand evidence about a topic. Witnesses to a historical event create primary sources. They include autobiographies, newspaper reports of the time, oral histories, photographs, and memoirs. A secondary source analyzes primary sources, and is one step or more removed from the event. Secondary sources include textbooks, encyclopedias, and commentaries.

The Einstein-Szilard Letter The letter written by Leo Szilard, Albert Einstein, and others, and signed by Einstein, helped convince the U.S. government to begin researching nuclear weapons. You can read the letter by visiting *www.atomicarchive.com/Docs/Begin /Einstein.shtml*

Eisenhower's "Atoms for Peace" Speech Eisenhower's 1953 speech to the United Nations changed the way many people thought about nuclear energy and its potential uses. You can read the speech by visiting *www.world-nuclear-university.org/about.aspx?id=8674 &terms=atoms%20for%20peace*

Hiroshima Photographs The bombing of Hiroshima caused massive destruction to a major Japanese city and killed thousands of innocent people. You can see photos of the aftermath by visiting *www.boston.com/bigpicture/2009/08/hiroshima_64_years_ago.html*

The Nuclear Non-Proliferation Treaty The Treaty on the Non-Proliferation of Nuclear Weapons helps prevent the creation of more nuclear weapons. You can view the treaty by visiting *www.un.org/en /conf/npt/2005/npttreaty.html*

The Nuclear Regulatory Commission The U.S. Nuclear Regulatory Commission creates guidelines for safety and inspects reactors to determine whether their licenses should be renewed. You can view some of the NRC's safety guidelines online by visiting *www.nrc.gov*

RESOURCES

Books

Benoit, Peter. *Nuclear Meltdowns*. New York: Children's Press, 2012.

Finkelstein, Norman. *Thirteen Days/Ninety Miles: The Cuban Missile Crisis*. Bloomington, IN: iUniverse, 2001.

Gray, Mike, and Ira Rosen. *The Warning: Accident at Three Mile Island: A Nuclear Omen for the Age of Terror*. New York: W. W. Norton & Company, 2003.

Kidd, J. S., and Renee A. Kidd. *Nuclear Power: The Study of Quarks and Sparks*. New York: Chelsea House Publishers, 2006.

Richardson, Hazel. *How to Split the Atom*. New York: Franklin Watts, 2001.

Tabak, John. *Nuclear Energy (Energy and the Environment)*. New York: Facts on File, 2009.

Web Sites

The Cold War Museum

http://coldwar.org/

This site offers a fascinating look at 45 years of Cold War history. It includes photos, video, artwork, and stories.

Photographs of Hiroshima and Nagasaki

www.gensuikin.org/english/photo.html

The site provides photographs and related stories of the aftermath of the Hiroshima and Nagasaki bombings.

Visit this Scholastic Web site for more information on the nuclear age:
www.factsfornow.scholastic.com

GLOSSARY

atoms (AT-uhmz) the tiniest parts of an element that still have all the properties of that element

blockade (blok-ADE) a closing off of an area, such as a port, to keep supplies from going in or out

climate change (KLYE-mit CHAYNJ) global warming and other changes in the weather and weather patterns that are happening because of human activity

excavations (ek-skuh-VAY-shuhnz) large holes dug in the earth to search for something buried, as in archeological research, or to prepare the ground for the construction of a building

fallout (FAWL-out) radioactive dust from a nuclear explosion

greenhouse gases (GREEN-hous GAS-iz) gases such as carbon dioxide and methane that contribute to the warming of Earth

kamikaze attacks (kah-mih-KAH-zee uh-TAKS) suicide attacks performed by Japanese pilots during World War II

lobbies (LAH-beez) groups of people who try to influence politicians on specific issues

meltdown (MELT-doun) the melting of the core of a nuclear reactor, which allows dangerous radiation to escape into the atmosphere

nuclear fission (NOO-klee-ur FISH-uhn) the splitting of the nucleus of an atom, which creates energy

nuclear reactors (NOO-klee-ur ree-AK-turz) large devices in a power station that produce nuclear power

nucleus (NOO-klee-uhs) the central part of an atom that is made up of neutrons and protons

proliferation (pruh-lif-uh-RAY-shuhn) excessive spread or increase

spent uranium (SPENT yu-RAY-nee-uhm) uranium that has already been used as fuel for a nuclear reactor

INDEX

Page numbers in *italics* indicate illustrations.

ABOUT THE AUTHOR

Peter Benoit is a graduate of Skidmore College in Saratoga Springs, New York. His degree is in mathematics. He has been a tutor and educator for many years. Peter has written more than two dozen books for Children's Press. He has written about ecosystems, disasters, and Native Americans, among other topics. He is also the author of more than 2,000 poems.

2/12